WHAT IS SHONEN JUMP?

The world of *SHONEN JUMP* is the birthplace of manga sensations Beet, Ichigo and Shô, as well as continuing hits *RUROUNI KENSHIN, SHAMAN KING, YU-GI-OH!, DRAGON BALL Z* and *THE PRINCE OF TENNIS*. Originating in Japan, each issue of Japan's *Weekly Shonen Jump* and *Monthly Shonen Jump* carries the decades-long tradition of Japanese comics propelled by vibrant art and intriguing storylines. Now that VIZ has brought *SHONEN JUMP* Magazine to the U.S., American readers can discover what millions of manga fans already know: no other comics anthology packs more action and adventure between its covers.

WHAT IS THE SHONEN JUMP GRAPHIC NOVEL LINE?

The SHONEN JUMP GRAPHIC NOVEL Line is the future of manga — it's the voice of the most exciting titles making the leap from Japan to the U.S.

Each manga title has the unique style and voice of its artist/creator. All of the manga are presented in the right-to-left format just as they are in Japan. This format allows the panels to be displayed as the artists intended, and adds authenticity and fun to the reader's experience.

So brace yourself for an amazing adventure in the third *SHONEN JUMP GRAPHIC NOVEL COMPILATION EDITION*. Here's a sample of the most intense action, nail-biting cliffhangers and coolest characters around. You're about to JUMP head first into the world of manga. Enjoy!

THE WORLD'S MOST POPULAR MANGA

SHONEN JUMP

GRAPHIC NOVELS

Managing Editor *Elizabeth Kawasaki*
Contributing Editor *Livia Ching*
Cover & Graphics Design *Veronica Casson*
Design Assistant *Izumi Hirayama*

Executive Vice President & Editor in Chief *Hyoe Narita*
Director of Production *Noboru Watanabe*
Editorial Director *Alvin Lu*
Senior Director of Licensing & Acquisitions *Rika Inouye*
Vice President of Sales *Joe Morici*
Vice President of Marketing *Liza Coppola*
Vice President of Strategic Development *Yumi Hoashi*
Publisher *Seiji Horibuchi*

BEET THE VANDEL BUSTER
English Adaptation *Shaenon K. Garrity*
Translation *Naomi Kokubo*
Touch-Up & Lettering *Mark McMurray*
Graphics & Cover Design *Sean Lee*
Editor *Richard Kadrey*

BLEACH
English Adaptation *Lance Caselman*
Translation *Joe Yamazaki*
Touch-Up Art & Lettering *Andy Ristaino*
Graphics & Cover Design *Sean Lee*
Editor *Kit Fox*

WHISTLE!
English Adaptation *Marv Wolfman*
Translation *Naomi Kokubo*
Touch-Up & Lettering *Jim Keefe*
Graphics & Cover Design *Sean Lee*
Editor *Eric Searleman*

DRAGON BALL
Editor *Jason Thompson*

DRAGON BALL Z
Editor *Jason Thompson*

HIKARU NO GO
Editor *Livia Ching*

KNIGHTS OF THE ZODIAC (SAINT SEIYA)
Editor *Shaenon K. Garrity*

NARUTO
Editor *Frances E. Wall*

ONE PIECE
Editor *Megan Bates*

THE PRINCE OF TENNIS
Editor *Michelle Pangilinan*

RUROUNI KENSHIN
Editor *Avery Gotoh*
Compilation Edition Editor *Kit Fox*

SHAMAN KING
Editor *Jason Thompson*

YU-GI-OH!
Editor *Jason Thompson*

YUYU HAKUSHO
Editor *Michelle Pangilinan*

www.shonenjump.com
EXPLANATION OF AGE RATINGS

ALL AGES Suitable for all ages. May contain some violence. Examples: *Beet the Vandel Buster, Dragon Ball Z, Hikaru no Go, The Prince of Tennis* and *Whistle!*

TEEN May contain violence, language, suggestive situations and alcohol or tobacco usage. Recommended for ages 13 and up. Examples: *Bleach, Dragon Ball, Knights of the Zodiac, Naruto, One Piece, Shaman King, Yu-Gi-Oh!* and *YuYu Hakusho.*

OLDER TEENS May contain graphic violence, language, suggestive situations, brief nudity and alcohol or tobacco usage. Recommended for ages 16 and up.

Example: *Rurouni Kenshin.*

THE WORLD'S MOST POPULAR MANGA

SHONEN JUMP

™

GRAPHIC NOVELS

CONTENTS

Welcome to the Century of Darkness where monsters (known in Beet's world as "Vandels") are as plentiful as cops at a Krispy Kreme. We meet Beet as he begins his training as a Buster, a warrior who specializes in monster smashing. Before long, Beet's scored himself a few points as a Buster, as well as a mortal enemy — Beltorze, the strongest, meanest, most dangerous Vandel of all.

But Beet has a secret. Five secrets, really: the indestructible weapons magically bestowed on him by the Zenon Army. Now, if Beet can only stay awake and alive long enough to learn to use them…

Bursting with action and laughs, **Beet the Vandel Buster** will lead readers down the road to nonstop adventures and excitement!

Beet

A young, inexperienced Vandel Buster who possesses the five saiga weapons of the Zenon Army, which gives him power he really can't quite control. Beet is an orphan raised by his friend Poala's family.

Poala

Beet's childhood friend and a fellow Vandel fighter. Beet plans to marry her someday, but Poala isn't so sure about that!

Beltorze

A violent, dangerous Vandel. He's the highest-ranked Vandel of all, and Beet's mortal enemy.

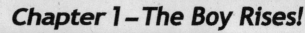

VZZZZ....

AS I'VE SAID TO YOU MANY TIMES, ONCE YOU'RE BRANDED, YOU CAN'T GO BACK TO A NORMAL CAREER.

...SURE YOU ABOUT THIS, REALLY...? BEET..?

GGHAK

...OKAY WITH THAT?

VZ VZ YOU'RE...

VZ

STARTING TODAY... I'M GONNA BE A VANDEL BUSTER!!!

TA-DA

000

GULP

I'VE ALREADY MADE UP MY MIND!!

ER... YUP! OF COURSE!

SHFF

Chapter 1 — The Boy

BEET
THE VANDEL BUSTER

GYAAA AAAH!!!

SIZZLE

N-NOT AT ALL!!

BRR   BRR

WASN'T IT PAINFUL?

TAP

...WHAT'S HE DOING?

I'LL SHOW THEM... RIGHT NOW!!

AL-ALL RIGHT...!!

GAH!!

THROB THROB

THROB

...

NO WAY! I FEEL AS IF I'VE BECOME A GROWN MAN AND IT FEELS GREAT!!

VICTORY!!

THESE MONSTERS ARE NOTHING BUT THE EVIL SERVANTS THEY PRODUCE FOR FUN...

CRUSS

DON'T FEAR US JUST BECAUSE WE FINISHED AN EASY JOB LIKE THAT.

...

ALSIDE

OUR JOB IS TO DESTROY THOSE WHO CONTROL THE MONSTERS.

BLUEZAM

LAIO

...THE BUSTERS' TRUE ENEMIES...

...ARE THE VANDELS!

THAT'S RIGHT. AFTER ALL...

ZENON

Hidden in darkness, one day they appeared on the surface of the EARTH, multiplying monsters and destroying the peace and order of human society. Years have passed since that day.

Vandels!! In this story, that's what we call evil creatures with magical powers.

GO GO GOTOON

...the Century of Dark- ness...

People call this seemingly endless era...

16

THANK YOU...
THEY ALMOST
BROKE THROUGH...
THANK YOU...

NO
PROBLEM
AT ALL!

SHHK

BUSINESS
AS USUAL.

HEE HEE...
THE ONLY
FRIENDLY
LOCAL IS
THE "GATE,"
HUH?

...

TH-
THAT
MEANS...

THEY'RE
NOT THE
KIND OF
MONSTERS
THAT COME
INTO BEING
NATURALLY.

THIRTY IRON
RHINOS...
THEY TRIED
TO OPEN
THE GATE.

H-HOW
WAS IT,
ZENON?

17

THE VANDEL BELTORZE...!!

HUBBUB

HUBBUB

S-SO HE'S COMING!!

THE "KING OF TRAGEDY" !!

THE RUMOR'S TRUE... HE'S NEARBY...

THAT POWER-FUL VANDEL...

SHHF

I'M GONNA HELP YOU...

ZENON !!

THAT'S WHY WE'RE HERE!

MUTTER MUTTER

CHATTER

D-DO YOU THINK YOU CAN DEFEAT HIM...?

18

GEEZ, THAT IDIOT KID'S SHOWN UP AGAIN TODAY!

...BEET!

TA-DA!

IT'S IRRITATING TO GET THE COLD SHOULDER FROM TOWNSPEOPLE, BUT THE FANATIC BELIEVERS ARE A PROBLEM, TOO.

IT'S NORMAL FOR KIDS TO IDOLIZE TOUGH GUYS. IT'S LIKE A FEVER. HE'LL COOL DOWN SOON ENOUGH...

CAN'T BE HELPED...

WHAT DO WE DO WITH THAT BEET? HE'S ALL OVER THEM...

THEN WHAT ARE YOU?

I'M NOT A BELIEVER, AND I'M NOT A FAN OF YOURS, LAIO!

A LONG-ANTICIPATED NEW WEAPON!!

19

HE'S RIGHT. WE'RE PROFESSIONALS, GOT IT?

THAT'S ALL.

OUR JOB ISN'T CHILD'S PLAY.

WHAT?

GO HOME, BEET.

BUT WHY, ZENON?

I FINALLY MADE THE CONTRACT WITH VANDEL BUSTERS.

LOOK!!

GRP

THAT'S NOT AN ISSUE.

AS OF TODAY, I'M A PRO...

...THE REAL THING!!

20

YOU SAID THAT TO THE KID?

SO I MADE THE CONTRACT, DESPITE THE EXCRUCIATING PAIN!!

IT WAS YOU, LAIO, WHO SAID, "I CAN'T PLAY WITH YOU, KID. COME BACK ONCE YOU'RE A BUSTER." RIGHT?

Y-YOU... YOU...?

ER... I DIDN'T EXPECT HIM TO TAKE IT SERIOUSLY...

MAKE ME ONE OF THE ZENON WARRIORS NOW!!!

OKAY!! LET ME JOIN YOU!

IDIOT!!

BA-CH AK

YOU...

...PO...

POALA...

HE'S A NEW KIND OF WEAPON, ALL RIGHT...

OOG...

OOO

OOO

OOO

OOO

ZHF

ZHF ZHF

I'M... HAVING...

...AN IMPORTANT CONVER- SATION...

I'D ALREADY MADE UP MY MIND TO BECOME A BUSTER SOMEDAY. SO WHAT'S THE DIFFERENCE?

...SHAD-DUP...

THRB THRB

WHAT'RE YOU THINKING? BINDING YOUR-SELF TO THE CONTRACT JUST LIKE THAT!

IDIOT!

IDIOT!

IDIOT!

...

HOW DO YOU THINK MY PARENTS WILL FEEL? THEY'VE LOOKED AFTER YOU SINCE YOUR PARENTS DIED.

BESIDES, ONCE I'M A TOP BUSTER, I'LL MARRY YOU!

I'M SURE YOUR PARENTS ARE GONNA LOVE IT.

IT'S ALL RIGHT. I PLAN TO BE THE STRONGEST, *THE FIRST-CLASS BUSTER* IN THE WORLD.

WHO'D MARRY YOU?!

AS IF!!

KA-POW

SO YOU'VE GOT NO WORRIES...

...RIGHT?

23

ALL RIGHT!

BAM

HMPH...

...WHY DOESN'T ANYONE BELIEVE ME?

IS IT BECAUSE I'M STILL ONLY LEVEL 1?

I'LL EARN MY PROMOTION POINTS BY DEFEATING MONSTERS, ONE AFTER THE OTHER!

POWW

I'M SURE I CAN RAISE MY LEVEL UP TO 10 IN NO TIME.

AFTER ALL, I'M "THE MAN WHO CAN FIGHT FOR THREE DAYS AND NIGHTS"!

SLLP

THAT'S RIGHT.

BEET IS A STRANGE CHILD.

HE SLEEPS ONLY ONCE EVERY THREE DAYS?

...?

24

IT'S ADVANTAGEOUS TO BE ABLE TO STAY ACTIVE FOR A LONG TIME WHEN PURSUING AN ENEMY OR GOING ON AN ADVENTURE...

HMPH. IN A WAY, THAT'S PERFECT FOR A BUSTER.

HE'S UP FOR THREE DAYS AND THEN SLEEPS FOR A WHOLE DAY... HE'S BEEN LIKE THAT FOR A LONG TIME. IT'S HOW HE'S BUILT, I GUESS.

WHEN ICICLE BATS PUT HOLES IN THE ROOF OF THE INN, HE FIXED IT IN THREE DAYS ON HIS OWN.

HE'D PLAY OR DO CHORES FOR THREE DAYS STRAIGHT.

IF A MONSTER ATTACKED HIM WHILE HE WAS ASLEEP, HE'D BE IN REAL TROUBLE.

RIGHT?

I'M NOT SO SURE! AFTER FIXING THAT ROOF, HE FELL ASLEEP WHILE HE WAS TAKING A BATH AND SLEPT THERE ALL DAY.

I MEANT TO RAISE THAT BOY TO LEAD A NORMAL LIFE, BUT...

I'M SORRY, ZENON.

...

BY THE TIME HE WOKE UP, HIS SKIN WAS TOTALLY WRINKLED.

...

25

LET ME CHECK UP ON HIM A BIT...

THUD

THANKS A LOT...

...LAIO.

IT'S THE LEAST I CAN DO.

YOU ALWAYS LET US STAY AT YOUR PLACE, EVERY TIME WE COME TO THE VILLAGE. IF YOU DIDN'T, WE'D HAVE TO CAMP OUT.

AH, BUT HOW TIRESOME...

...COULD IT MEAN HE HAS...

...THAT MUCH MORE POWER?

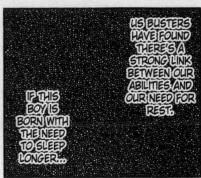

US BUSTERS HAVE FOUND THERE'S A STRONG LINK BETWEEN OUR ABILITIES, AND OUR NEED FOR REST.

IF THIS BOY IS BORN WITH THE NEED TO SLEEP LONGER...

HEY!! LET GO! FIGHT ME FACE TO FACE!!

...

SPLOOSH

SPLOOSH SPLOOSH

GYAAAAH!!!

OU-OU-OUCH!!!

WHAM

WHAM WHAM

DIDN'T I JUST TELL YOU? YOU CAN'T USE THE SPEAR LIKE THAT WHEN YOU ATTACK...

27

NEVER!!

N-NO!!

IF YOU AGREE NOT TO BECOME ONE...

...I'LL HELP YOU OUT!

I'M TELLING YOU, YOU'RE BETTER OFF NOT BECOMING A BUSTER!!

HOW CAN— IT HURTS LIKE CRAZY!

BUT—

BUT—

...

LOOSEN UP!

FWOOO

LOOSEN UP FIRST!

IF YOU TIGHTEN YOUR MUSCLES, THE TEETH WILL SINK FURTHER.

HOLD THE NECK OF THE SPEAR AND, USING THE POINT, CUT THE MOUTH OFF THE SHELL FROM BEHIND!

AHH... HE'S RIGHT!

IT'S NOT AS PAINFUL AS BEFORE!!

PLOP

SLICE

SU SU

IT'S THE FIRST TIME I EVER DEFEATED A MONSTER!

I-- I DID IT!!

!!

I DID IT!!

YIPPEE!!

SLOSH

SLOSH

SLOSH

THANKS! I DIDN'T EXPECT YOU TO GIVE ME ADVICE, ZENON!!

YOU IDIOT! YOU GET THE FEWEST PROMOTION POINTS FROM THE BITING CLAMS!!

SO HOW MANY PROMOTION POINTS DO I GET FROM THIS ONE?

AM I UP TO LEVEL 5 OR SOMETHING LIKE THAT?

...!

HUH

I'LL SURPRISE YOU BY GETTING STRONGER WHILE YOU GUYS ARE STILL IN THE VILLAGE!!

WELL, NONETHELESS, I'LL DO MY BEST!

...A LONGER ROAD THAN I EXPECTED, HUH?

...

YOU'LL BE LUCKY TO REACH LEVEL 3 EVEN AFTER YOU KILL OFF A HUNDRED OF THEM.

WHY DO YOU WANT TO BECOME A BUSTER SO MUCH?

WELL? HOW COME?

...

BY "FIGHTING THREE DAYS AND NIGHTS," HUH?

YOU DON'T GIVE UP, DO YOU?

IT'S BECAUSE...

HUH?

I WANNA BE A BUSTER LIKE THAT!!

YEAH! ZENON WARRIORS ARE THE BUSTERS OF JUSTICE, GETTING RID OF THE VANDELS AND PROTECTING HUMANS, RIGHT?

...I WANNA BE COOL LIKE YOU GUYS, ZENON!

...LIKE US?

JUSTICE... HOO BOY...

YOU'VE SEEN THE WAY THE VILLAGERS LOOK AT US, HAVEN'T YOU? WE RISK OUR LIVES EVERY DAY, BUT NOBODY LIKES US.

YOU WON'T LAST LONG IDOLIZING THE JOB OR THINKING IT'S ALL FUN.

TO BE HONEST, IT'S NOT ALL THAT COOL.

BEET, KILLING VANDELS AND MONSTERS IS A BUSTER'S JOB. SIMPLE AS THAT.

IT'S UNDERSTANDABLE.

ALTHOUGH OUR ENEMIES AREN'T HUMAN, WE AREN'T TOO DIFFERENT FROM ASSASSINS.

IN A WAY, WE'RE TREATED LIKE THE VANDELS.

OR DO YOU WANT TO BRAG ABOUT KILLING THE MONSTERS?

SO ARE YOU FIGHTING FOR MONEY?

THAT'S NOT TRUE!

WE CAN'T CALL... WHAT WE DO... JUSTICE.

...THAT'S TRUE, BUT...

YOU'RE WORKING HARD FOR THE SAKE OF THE VILLAGERS AND PEOPLE AROUND THE WORLD!!

I DON'T THINK SO!

THAT'S WHAT'S CALLED JUSTICE!!

DON'T YOU KNOW?

SHEEN

HIYAAH!!

ZENON...

...

I'M ALL PREPARED, SO WHY DON'T YOU GO BACK AND SLEEP.

OKAY! NOW THAT I KNOW WHAT TO DO, LET ME CLEAN UP THIS POND!!

...

I'VE GOT THIS FEELING HE'S REALLY GONNA CHANGE SOME-DAY...

THANKS TO ZENON'S ADVICE, I CAN EASILY DESTROY BITING CLAMS NOW!

HEE HEE HEE...

SPLSH
SPLSH

GYAHH

NUTS!! I'M FADING...

BYAAAA

ONLY ONES LEFT ARE...

SPLSH

HUH...

HUH...

SPLSH

OH, YEAH... TODAY'S... MY DAY TO SLEEP...

NO... SHOULDN'T... SLEEP HERE...

DIZZY...

SPLASH

THEY'LL BITE ME... ALL OVER...

...

...HE'S COMING!

...!?

...YOU'RE...!!

SMIRK

36

...IT WON'T LAST.

CREAK

BAM

CREAK

CREAK

SORRY... I'LL BE BROKEN THROUGH...

...BY A SINGLE...

...VANDEL!!

RRRIP

I SLEPT IN THE WATER ALL DAY AGAIN...

THIS IS NOT GOOD.

SPLASH

BLOOP

BLOOP

...

RRUMBLE

CHK

40

THE VANDEL'S INCREDIBLE... BUT WHAT'RE THOSE THINGS? THOSE WEAPONS THEY'RE HOLDING?

AH! WOW!

NO OTHER BUSTER HAS CORNERED ME SO FAR...

NO VANDEL'S CORNERED ME.

CROWN SHIELD!

CYCLONE GUNNER!

BURNING LANCE!

IT'S USUALLY HIDDEN INSIDE THE BUSTER'S BODY. IT'S THE LAST WEAPON A BUSTER USES, UNSHEATHED ONLY IN TIMES OF GREAT DANGER...

A SAIGA IS A BUSTER'S STRONGEST DEFENSE.

SAIGA?

SAIGA!

THIS IS THE FIRST TIME WE'VE BROUGHT OUT ALL FIVE OF OUR SAIGA.

THE VILLAGE?

THIS IS IT, BEL-TORZE!

WE WON'T LET YOU TOUCH THAT VILLAGE!!

SO A SAIGA... COMES RIGHT OUT OF THE BODY!?

45

‼⁉

I'M NOT INTERESTED IN THAT TO BEGIN WITH.

THE VILLAGE, INDEED...

HA HA HA... NOT A PROBLEM.

WH-WHAT!?

ALL I WANT IS YOUR FIVE HEADS.

ANY PLACE WOULD'VE BEEN FINE, SO LONG AS YOU WERE THERE!

WE VANDELS PUT A PRICE ON THE HEADS OF STRONG BUSTERS!

BY TAKING FIVE OF YOUR LIVES, I CAN GET ONE OF THESE.

I HEAR HUMANS DO THE SAME THING.

...HE'D FLATTEN THE VILLAGE!

F-FOR THAT LITTLE CHIP OF GLASS...

IT'S A STAR. DESTROYING A WHOLE COUNTRY WON'T EARN A SINGLE STAR.

46

ISN'T IT AN ECSTATIC MOMENT FOR A WARRIOR?

WHAT DO YOU THINK? ISN'T THAT TOUCHING TO LEARN THAT YOU'RE VALUED SO HIGHLY?

IN OTHER WORDS, YOUR DEATHS ARE WORTH MORE THAN AN ENTIRE COUNTRY.

GOT IT?

SNAP!!

BEL-TORZE... IT'S UNFOR-GIVABLE!!

WE'LL KILL YOU!!!

BEET SAW IT!!

THE DEATH MATCH...

...BETWEEN THE VANDEL AND THE BUSTERS, TWO SIDES AT THE HEIGHT OF THEIR POWERS.

48

IT'S AS IF THEY'RE IN ANOTHER WORLD!

T-TOO INCREDIBLE... NO WONDER THEY NEVER TOOK ME SERIOUSLY...

FOR BEET, LEVEL 1...

...IT LOOKED LIKE A MATCH AMONG THE GODS IN THE HEAVENS!!!

THEY'LL WIN!!

YES!! IT LOOKS LIKE ZENON'S TEAM IS STRONGER!

49

50

TO BE CONTINUED IN BEET THE VANDEL BUSTER, VOL.1

Cleaning up the afterlife, one spirit at a time!

chigo Kurosaki has always been able to see ghosts, but this ability doesn't change his life nearly as much as his close encounter with Rukia Kuchiki, a Soul Reaper and member of the mysterious Soul Society.

While fighting a Hollow, an evil spirit that preys on humans who display psychic energy, Rukia attempts to lend Ichigo some of her powers so that he can save his family. But much to her surprise, Ichigo absorbs every last drop of her energy. Now an official Soul Reaper himself, Ichigo quickly learns that the world he inhabits is one full of dangerous spirits, and along with Rukia — who is slowly regaining her powers — it's Ichigo's job to both protect the innocent from Hollows and to help the spirits themselves find peace.

Ichigo "Strawberry" Kurosaki

- Likes slim fit shirts and pants

- Favorite celebrities are Mike Ness and Al Pacino

- Person he respects most is William Shakespeare

Rukia Kuchiki

- Likes climbing to high places

- Likes rabbit-related items

- Enjoys horror manga

Orihime Inoue

- Likes flower prints and comedy

- Daydreams a lot

- Puts butter on baked sweet potatoes

Yasutora "Chad" Sado

- Likes loud shirts, neck always open

- Likes small animals

- Likes tomatoes

2:23 A.M., FRIDAY   KARAKURA TOWN

I FEEL IT HERE...

STRANGE...

I SENSE ENORMOUS SPIRIT ENERGY...

1. STRAWBERRY & THE SOUL REAPERS

AND SO FELL THE SWORD OF FATE.

1. STRAWBERRY & THE SOUL REAPERS

WHAT THE ...!?

YOU COME HERE, STOMP LI'L YAMA IN THE FACE, AND ORDER US OUT LIKE WE WAS DOGS?!

YOU CRAZY, PUNK?

GOT A DEATH-WISH?

SPEAK!

ICHIGO "STRAWBERRY" KUROSAKI:

15 YEARS OLD
HAIR: ORANGE
EYES: BROWN

OCCUPATION: HIGH SCHOOL STUDENT

SAY SOMETHING, YOU...

SPECIAL SKILL:

THAT GUY'S A TOTAL STONE-COLD PSYCHO!

MESS WITH HIM, AND HE'LL KILL YOU!!

THIS IS MESSED UP...

REAL MESSED UP...

THAT'S ONE BLOOD-THIRSTY BERRY HEAD.

GULP

HE DROPPED LI'L TOSHI!!

WHUMP

LORD BUD-DHA...

ALL OF YOU CHUMPS, LOOK AT THAT!!

SHUT UP!!

A-DA-DA-DA-

MRPF

AN OFFERING FOR SOME DEAD KID?

UMM...

YOU, SMELLY LOOKIN' DUDE!!

YOU TELL ME!!

WHAT'S THAT!?

HUH?

M-ME?

SMELLY?

QUESTION ONE!!

URK

LI'L MITCH?!

QUESTION TWO!!!

YOU OKAY, LI'L MITCH?!

LI'L MITCH!!

KA-

CHECK OUT THE BRAIN ON SMELLY!!

GON

WE KNOCKED IT OVER WITH OUR SKATE...

DAT'S 'CUZ...

DA-DA-DA-DA-DA-DA

BOARDS?

IS THAT SO?

ICHIGO "STRAWBERRY" KUROSAKI: 15 YEARS OLD

HAIR COLOR: ORANGE

EYE COLOR: BROWN

OCCUPATION: HIGH SCHOOL STUDENT

WHY IS THAT VASE...

LYING ON ITS SIDE?

SPECIAL SKILL...

READ THIS WAY

NO PROBLEM.

YEAH, YOU REST IN PEACE.

OKAY.

THANK YOU.

NOW I CAN REST PEACEFULLY.

I'LL BRING --

FRESH FLOWERS SOON.

IT'S TRUE. I CAN SEE AND TALK WITH GHOSTS.

I WAS BORN WITH THE ABILITY TO SEE THE SOULS OF THE DEAR DEPARTED.

MY FAMILY RUNS THE LOCAL CLINIC.

WE'RE ENTRUSTED WITH THE LIVES OF THE LIVING.

MAYBE THERE'S SOME CONNECTION THERE...

YOU'RE LATE!!!

I'M HOME...

BAM

KREET

HYOOOOOOO

I'M IN PERMANENT DENIAL.

IF I REFUSE TO BELIEVE IN THEM, IT'S LIKE THEY DON'T EXIST.

NOT ME.

I'D LOVE TO SEE ONE CLEARLY.

WE'RE BOUND TO BE A LITTLE ENVIOUS OF YOU, ICHIGO. THEY'RE JUST BLURRY SHAPES TO ME.

HUH? BUT YOU SEE THEM TOO, KARIN!

DUMMY.

ONLY DADDY CAN'T.

I DON'T BELIEVE IN GHOSTS.

YOU'RE NOT MAKING MONEY OFF MY GRIEF!!

I'M NOT A FREAK-SHOW!!

DAMMIT, KARIN!!

CHERRY BLOSSOM WATCHING WAS LAST MONTH, RIGHT?

"WANT TO FLIRT WITH GHOSTS WHILE BEING CARESSED BY THE FIRST BREEZE OF SUMMER?

A LIMITED ENGAGEMENT FOR THE MONTH OF MAY, THE KARUIZAWA GHOST PICNIC."

SO --

HERE'S MY LATEST PLAN.

FOR REAL...

I'VE BEEN ABLE TO SEE GHOSTS FOR AS LONG AS I CAN REMEMBER.

I SEE THE DEAD AS WELL AS I SEE THE LIVING.

?

K

BAM

BA

GR

DROPPED YOUR GUARD!!

WHAT?!

HE TALKS ABOUT STUFF LIKE THAT WITH YOU!!

ICHIGO'S BEEN UNDER A LOT OF PRESSURE LATELY!

HE TOLD ME MORE GHOSTS THAN EVER HAVE BEEN HAUNTING HIM.

HE'S FED UP!

WHAT'D I DO?!

IT'S YOUR FAULT, DAD.

HE LEFT.

THAT'S IT! I'M GOING TO BED!!

TUMP TUMP TUMP

OH!

ICHIGO!!

FIRST, TAKE DOWN THAT STUPID MEMORIAL PICTURE.

MASAKI FOREVER

AW...

MOTHER... MAYBE IT'S BECAUSE THEY'VE HIT PUBERTY, BUT OUR DAUGHTERS TREAT ME LIKE DIRT...

WHAT SHOULD I DO?

!!!!

I WOULDN'T BRING MY PROBLEMS TO YOU EITHER.

YOU'RE OVER 40 YET POSSESS THE EMOTIONAL MATURITY OF A PRESCHOOLER.

I'LL TAKE SOME SUPPER UP TO HIS ROOM LATER.

THAT BOY... WHY DOESN'T HE COME TO ME WITH HIS PROBLEMS?

ARE YOU SERIOUS?

THE EXISTENCE OF SOUL REAPERS...

...

A BLACK SWALLOWTAIL BUTTERFLY?

WHERE'D IT COME FROM?

FLUTTER

GEEZ...

WHY IS MY FAMILY SO WEIRD?

SL AM

15

HAD NEVER CROSSED MY MIND.

WHAT THE...

SH

AAA

TP TP TP TP TP TP

GWOOO

TUMP ooo

IT'S CLOSE ...!

HOW'S THAT FOR CLOSE, JERK?!

WHACK

HECK YEAH I CAN SEE YOU...

HUH?

STOP YAMMER-ING!

YOU... YOU CAN SEE ME?!!

AND... YOU KICKED ME!

WHAT'S CLOSE?! THE SAFE? IS THAT BURGLAR-SPEAK OR SOMETHING?!

? ? ? ?

PSH!!

PRETTY COCKY FOR A BURGLAR, AINTCHA?!

CRA

HOW CAN I BE QUIET WHEN I'M SUBDUING INTRUDERS?!

QUIET, BOY!

STOP JUMPING AROUND UP HERE!!

GOFPH!

DOM

WHAT?

LOOK AT WHO?

HUH?

LOOK AT THIS! WHERE'S OUR HOME SECURITY !?

IT IS NO USE.

THE CHICK IN THE SAMURAI GEAR...

HUH?

SOUL REAPER.

I'M A...

NORMAL PEOPLE CANNOT SEE ME.

KER SPLASH

NEAR...

MUCH SPIRIT ENERGY...

...NEAR BY...

TWITCH

.....!

RIP
TEAR
SHRED

KER-CHIKS

DRIP

PLOP

DRIP

GADUMP

THAT MAKES SENSE...

TO VANQUISH AN EVIL SPIRIT.

YOU CAME ALL THE WAY FROM THIS **SOUL SOCIETY** THING...

YOU'RE A **SOUL REAPER**, AND...

ICHIGO HIT ME HARD. DADDY'S UPSET.

THERE, THERE.

YOU ASKED FOR IT.

THAT'S YOUR STORY?

KUROSAKI CLINIC

THIS IS **KIDÔ**, THE DEMON WAY, A HIGH-LEVEL SPELL ONLY A SOUL REAPER CAN CAST!

HEH HEH... IT IS USELESS TO STRUGGLE!

CRAZY GIRL... WHAT DID YOU DO?!

DOOMP!

OW OW OW OW OW!!

TUMBLE

I WOULD KILL AN INSOLENT FOOL LIKE YOU, BUT THE PROVISIONAL SPIRIT LAW FORBIDS UNAUTHORIZED EXECUTIONS.

YET YOU DARE TO CALL ME "LITTLE SNOT?"

DESPITE MY APPEARANCE, I HAVE LIVED **TEN** OF YOUR LIVES!

CHOP

W-WAIT...

AND THIS...

....!

BE GRATE-FUL, **LITTLE SNOT!**

I WILL LET YOU OFF WITH A MINOR CASE OF PARALYSIS THIS TIME.

HERR-GGG!!!

FREAKIN' WANNABE SAMURAI...

WHAT AWAITS YOU IS NOT HELL.

IT IS THE SOUL SOCIETY.

DO NOT PRESUME.

NO... N...

I...

DON'T WANT TO GO TO HELL!

WHA...?

IT IS A RESTFUL PLACE.

UNLIKE HELL...

WHAT...

WHAT HAP-PENED?

WHERE'S THE GHOST?

...NO LONGER SEEMS NECES-SARY.

TO ASK IF YOU BELIEVE ME OR NOT...

YOU CALL IT "PASSING ON" IN YOUR LANGUAGE.

IT IS ONE OF THE DUTIES OF A SOUL REAPER.

I SENT HIM TO THE SOUL SOCIETY.

I PERF-ORM-ED KONSÔ,

THE SOUL FUN-ERAL.

NOW...

IN THIS REALM, THERE ARE TWO TYPES OF SOULS.

I WILL EXPLAIN SO THAT EVEN A BRAT LIKE YOU CAN UNDERSTAND.

BE SILENT AND LISTEN.

71

NOW THE OTHER TYPE...

WE CALL "HOLLOWS."

HOLLOWS ATTACK THE LIVING AND THE DEAD INDISCRIMINATELY, AND DEVOUR THEIR SOULS.

HOLLOW

BAD SPIRIT

HOLLOWS ARE "EVIL SPIRITS."

THE FIRST TYPE ARE THE "WHOLES," THE NORMAL SPIRITS.

THE GHOSTS YOU KNOW ARE OF THIS TYPE.

WHOLE

GOOD SPIRIT

LET US CONTINUE...

MONSIEUR GÉNÉRAL.

WHAT THE...?! YOU TOOK ADVANTAGE OF MY HELPLESSNESS!

HEY!!

HMMM...

WHY DOES YOUR DRAWING SUCK SO BAD?

ANY QUESTIONS SO FAR?

WE SOUL REAPERS HAVE TWO PRINCIPLE DUTIES...

72

FIRST, TO CONDUCT **WHOLES** TO THE SOUL SOCIETY BY MEANS OF KONSÔ...

KONSÔ

SOUL SOCIETY

WHICH IS MY MISSION NOW.

AND SECOND...

TO VAPORIZE HOLLOWS.

KAPOW!!

THERE IS.

YOU MEAN THERE'S A HOLLOW AROUND HERE NOW?

HANG ON.

?

WIPING MOUSTACHE OFF ON FLOOR

WHA... WHY NOT?

WHAT'S THE...

I HAVE NOT BEEN ABLE TO SENSE ITS PRESENCE FOR SOME TIME NOW.

ACT-UALLY... THAT IS...

ARE YOU STUPID!?

DON'T STAND THERE YAPPING!

GO VAPORIZE IT!

VNDOOOON

WHAT'S WRONG?!

WHAT'S WRONG?

THAT BLOOD-CURD-LING HOWL?

WHAT WAS THAT?

HEY, SOUL REAPER!!

HEY!

LIKE SOME FORCE OBSTRUCT-ING MY SENSES...

AAAH!!

...WHAT WAS...

...THAT?

GWAAOOOA

BLOOD-CURD-LING HOWL?

MAYBE...

AAOOUUOOO

WHAT IS IT I'M SENSING !?

BUT... IT'S LIKE I'M HEARING IT THROUGH SOME UNSEEN FILTER.

THAT WAS...

THE CRY OF A HOLLOW !!

I HEARD IT !!

...HEARD THE HOWL BEFORE I SENSED IT!?

THIS ONE HAVE...

BUT HOW COULD...

THAT HORRIBLE NOISE WAS THE HOWL OF A HOLLOW !?

HEY! WHERE YOU GOING !?

DASH!

THAT WAS YUZU!

CRASH!! AAAH!

!!

UNDO YOUR SPELL!!

NOW!!

HOLD UP!! THAT'S MY FAMILY BEING ATTACKED!!

I AM GOING TO KILL IT!!

STAY HERE!!

YES!

KER-ICHACK

YOU'LL ONLY SUCCEED IN ADDING TO THE BODY COUNT!

BE QUIET AND LEAVE THIS TO ME!

UNDERSTAND?!

DON'T BE A FOOL!!

THERE IS NOTHING YOU CAN DO!

WHAT...

I DID NOT SENSE IT UNTIL NOW...

THIS SPIRIT ENERGY?!

GWOOOO!!

...ARE YOU OKAY?

ICHIGO...

I....

WHAT IS HAPPENING TO ME !?

KARIN !!

THEN IT WENT FOR ME AND YUZU... SO FAST...

...I THOUGHT... HAD TO WARN...

ICHIGO...

...IT HAPPENED SO FAST...

DAD'S BACK EXPLODED AND HE FELL...

GOOD...

...IT HASN'T COME THIS WAY...

THAT CANNOT BE !!

HE BROKE THE KIDÔ BY HIS OWN POWER ?!

Impossible!!

WAIT!!

WHAT IS HE...?

YUZU!!

DAD!!

WHAM

80

HOLLOW!!

IT'S A...

IT...

82

WHEN SHE SAID **EVIL SPIRIT**, I THOUGHT IT'D LOOK HUMAN...

...BUT IT'S A MONSTER!!

THIS IS BAD! REALLY BAD!

WHY AM I SHAKING?!

TREMBLE TREMBLE TREMBLE TREMBLE

B BOOM

B BOOM B BOOM B BOOM

B BOOM BOOM

I'VE SEEN TONS OF GHOSTS!

IT'S JUST ANOTHER ONE!!

I'M NOT AFRAID OF THAT THING!!

ICHIGO
...!

YUZU
!!

AAARRRGH!

WAP

THE HOLLOW HAS NOT EATEN ANY OF YOUR FAMILY'S SOULS YET!

STAY CALM, BOY!

SKR

SH

YUZU!

YOU OKAY!?

SHAKE SHAKE

SO WHY'D THAT THING ATTACK MY FAMILY...

YOU SAID THE HOLLOWS ATTACK PEOPLE TO EAT THEIR SOULS!?

WAIT!

NOT EVEN THE SOUL OF YOUR FATHER -- WHO LIES ON THE FLOOR!

IT HASN'T!

OR BREAK A BINDING SPELL BEFORE...

I HAVE NEVER KNOWN A HUMAN WHO COULD SEE A SOUL REAPER...

I HAVE NEVER HEARD OF A HUMAN WITH SO MUCH SPIRIT ENERGY...

WHAT'S THAT MEAN?

HOLLOWS ARE DRAWN TO HIGH LEVELS OF SPIRIT ENERGY...

GA

GR

BUT THEY ALSO ATTACK OPPORTUNISTICALLY.

I BELIEVE HE WAS LOOKING...

FOR YOU!

!

KRERK

WHAT?!

HE WAS AFTER ME?!

HR RRR

HR RRR

THAT IS NOT WHAT I MEANT...

WAIT...

MY DAD'S DYING OVER THERE...

KARIN...

AND YUZU BLEEDING...

ALL OF THIS...

ALL THIS...

WAS 'CAUSE OF ME?!

SOUL REAPER!

...OF YOU!!

I'VE HAD ENOUGH...

READ THIS WAY

I FAILED TO GUARD MY FLANK...

HOW CARE-LESS.

SHAME-FUL...

KOOSH

UNH...

GRA

RRR

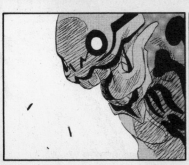

HEY...

UGLY...

YOU WANT MY SOUL?

90

TO BE CONTINUED IN BLEACH, VOL.1

Banned from his school's soccer team for being too short, Shô Kazamatsuri decides there's only one thing left to do: switch schools!

But even a change in scenery doesn't help the David Beckham wannabe. On campus, he is mistakenly introduced to everyone as a hotshot soccer player. When the truth is revealed, Shô drops out of school to train on his own.

Alone, the spunky teenager must work twice as hard to make his dreams come true. He wants to play soccer so bad he's willing to hustle day and night to make it happen.

Packed with action, humor and teenage kicks, *Whistle!* is a must-read for dreamers (and soccer fans) of all ages!

Shô Kazamatsuri

No one loves soccer more than this guy. He's an indefatigable spark plug who's an inspiration

Kô Kazamatsuri

Shô's older brother. A handsome guy who pays the rent by working for a host club (bar).

Ms. Yûko Katori

A teacher at Josui Junior High School. She mistakenly introduces Shô around campus as a hotshot soccer player

Tatsuya Mizuno

The best player on Josui's soccer squad, he becomes friends with Shô when he realizes they both share a passion for soccer

HEN THE WHISTLE BLOWS...
ET READY FOR ACTION!
ONLY $7.99 EACH
WHISTLE!
SHONEN JUMP GRAPHIC NOVEL
Story & Art by
Daisuke Higuchi
volume 1
volume 2
Vol. 1 on sale now!
WHISTLE!
Vol.2 available Nov. 9th!
SHONEN JUMP
GRAPHIC NOVELS
ON SALE AT
www.shonenjump.
Also available at your loc
bookstore, comic store an
Suncoast Motion Picture Com
COMIC SHOP LOCATOR SERVICE
888-COMIC-BOOK
888-266-4226
VIZ
WHISTLE! © 1998 by DAISUKE HIGUCHI / SHUEISHA Inc.

OFFENSE AND DEFENSE FROM THE 40 DEGREE.
VICTORY
DRAW
IT'S BEEN FOUR YEARS SINCE DORHA.
FRANCE
BATTLE WHERE DREAMS ARE AT STAKE.
STAGE.1
BREAK THROUGH
-BREAK THROUGH THE WALL-
EMBARRASSMENT
DEFEAT
DESPAIR
ASIA PRELIMINARY FINALS

DON'T LET GO OF THE DREAM!!

BELIEVE!

NEVER HESITATE!

BELIEVE IN YOUR OWN STRENGTH!!

IF YOU BELIEVE, THEN YOUR DREAMS ...

WILL COME TRUE WITHOUT FAIL! ...

NO MATTER THE SITUATION...

...FIGHT INSTEAD OF RUNNING AWAY!

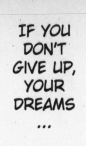

STAGE.1
BREAK THROUGH
-BREAK THROUGH THE WALL-

● INTRODUCTION ●

SOCCER IS A SPORT IN WHICH THE PLAYER'S TEAM STEALS THE BALL FROM THE OPPONENT'S TEAM THEN PASSES IT FROM PLAYER TO PLAYER UNTIL IT IS SHOT INTO THE OTHER TEAM'S GOAL. IT MAY SOUND EASY, BUT YOUR OPPONENTS WILL INTERFERE, MAKING IT DIFFICULT TO SCORE.

TO MAKE A GOAL, TEAMS ESTABLISH POSITIONS, INITIATE PASSES, SET UP COMPLICATED FORMATIONS AND TRY TO OUT-MANEUVER OPPONENTS.

THESE DAYS, THE PLAYERS, EXCLUDING GOALKEEPERS, CHANGE POSITIONS SO RAPIDLY AND CONSTANTLY THAT IT'S OFTEN HARD TO KEEP TRACK OF WHO IS POSITIONED WHERE. SINCE, UNLIKE BASEBALL, PLAYERS' POSITIONS ARE NOT FIXED, IT IS NOT NECESSARY TO KNOW WHERE THEY ARE AS YOU WATCH THEM PLAY. ALL YOU NEED TO DO IS KEEP IN MIND WHICH PLAYER TAKES WHAT POSITION WITHIN A FORMATION SUCH AS 4-4-2 OR 3-5-2.

BEYOND THAT, FOCUS ON FIGURING OUT HOW TO GAIN POINTS AND WHEN TO STEAL THE BALL. YOU MUST NOT ONLY WATCH THE GOAL BUT ALSO THE PROCESS OF GETTING THERE.

YOU WILL ENJOY SOCCER IF YOU CAN UNDERSTAND, AS AN EXAMPLE, THAT JOE'S GOAL WAS THE RESULT OF YAMAGUCHI'S PASS-CUT, OR THAT THE GOAL WAS POSSIBLE BECAUSE OF THE LAST PASS.

SOCCER ALLOWS PLAYERS TO USE ANY PART OF THEIR BODIES EXCEPT FOR THEIR HANDS. USING VARIOUS PARTS OF A PLAYER'S LEG, APPLYING DIVERSE INTENSITIES AS WELL AS DIFFERENT ANGLES, ALLOWS FOR A GREAT MANY WAYS TO PASS A BALL. ADDING BOTH LEGS AND FEET AS WELL AS YOUR HEAD, AND YOU'LL FIND IT IMPOSSIBLE TO COUNT HOW MANY WAYS A PLAYER CAN MAKE A PASS. ISN'T IT ALREADY EXCITING TO THINK ABOUT IT?

--TATSUYA WATANABE (WINNING RUN)

105

GOTTA ADMIT, YOU'RE A GOOD KID. ♥

AW, YOU JUST NEEDED SOMEONE TO GET YOU ORGANIZED.

STILL, I CAN'T BELIEVE YOU WANTED TO TRANSFER SCHOOLS AND LIVE WITH ME. BUT, STILL ...

... YOU'VE BEEN A REAL HELP.

CLEANING, DOING THE LAUNDRY AND THE COOKING ...

HOPE SO.

... WILL HAVE A FUN SOCCER TEAM.

I HOPE THAT THE NEXT SCHOOL ...

OH!

WHOOM

SEE YA. GOTTA GO.

SKRATCH

HOW EMBARRASSING ...

GEEZ ...

JOSUI JUNIOR
HIGH SCHOOL

WHOOSH WHOOSH

FWIP FWIP

WHEW!

UNHHHH

WHOOM

WHIIIP

...

UMM, EXCUSE...

2-A

AHH, HERE WE ARE.

OH?

TRANS-FERRING WAS MY IDEA.

BUT SINCE YOUR HOME ADDRESS IS WITHIN THIS SCHOOL DISTRICT, IT SHOULDN'T BE A PROBLEM. STILL...

...I ASSUME THIS IS YOUR PARENTS' WISH?

PERHAPS BECAUSE THEY REQUIRE ALL STUDENTS TO LIVE IN THEIR DORMITORY.

NO.

I MUST SAY WE'RE SURPRISED ANYONE WOULD TRANSFER HERE FROM A PRIVATE SCHOOL LIKE MUSASHINOMORI. THAT PLACE IS KNOWN FOR ITS ACADEMIC AND ATHLETIC ACHIEVE-MENTS.

SKREEEEK

YES, COME IN.

MS. KATORI, I BROUGHT THE TRANSFER STUDENT, SHŌ KAZAMATSURI.

NOK NOK

P-O-P

Welcome!

SHŌ KAZAMATSURI

IN ON IT!

HEH HEH

REALLY? I'M SO PROUD OF YOU...

146 CM.

...YOU'RE SMALLER THAN I THOUGHT. HOW TALL ARE YOU?

WELL...

GRIPPP

ER...

I'M YOUR TEACHER, YŪKO KATORI. HOW DO YOU DO? ♡

HUH?!

OUR TEAM'S BEEN CALLED JOSUI JUNIOR HIGH'S BIGGEST BURDEN, BUT NOW THAT...

SORRY TO INTERRUPT YOUR LUNCH.

STOMP

BY THE WAY, I'M THE ADVISOR FOR OUR SOCCER TEAM.

COME... SIT DOWN FOR THE LESSON.

I AM SO EXCITED.

IT'S SO INCREDIBLE THAT YOU TRANSFERRED FROM MUSASHI-NOMORI AND THEIR FAMOUS SOCCER TEAM...

LET'S TRY OUR BEST, GUYS!!

...IT'S TIME FOR THE AFTER SCHOOL ACTIVITY. ♡

HUH? REGULAR?

ALL RIGHT, SHŌ...

...WE'VE GOT A REGULAR FROM MUSASHINOMORI, THE TOKYO TOURNAMENT DOESN'T HAVE TO BE A DREAM ANY MORE!

TA-

DA!

HOW DO I TELL THEM I WAS JUST IN THE THIRD TEAM?

YAYYYY

HE'S GOOD -- MUCH BETTER THAN THE OTHERS.

HE'S MUSASHI-NOMORI GOOD.

OOPS!

WHAT'S YOUR NAME?

ER...

YES?

YŪSUKE OF SECOND YEAR.

WHUPP

HE'S AN EXCEPTIONAL PLAYER. MUSASHINOMORI EVEN TRIED TO RECRUIT HIM-- IT'S A MYSTERY WHY HE CAME HERE INSTEAD.

REALLY?

GOOD EYE, SHŌ! YOU'VE ALREADY SPOTTED TATSUYA!

OH, YOU MEAN, MIZUNO? HE'S TATSUYA MIZUNO OF SECOND YEAR.

HE'S A MIDFIELDER, BUT HE CAN HANDLE ANY POSITION.

YŪSUKE, WHO'S THAT INCREDIBLE GUY?

...THAT'S LIKE A COMPLETELY DIFFERENT WORLD FROM US--

YOU'RE FROM MUSASHINOMORI...

POLITE? BUT, YOU...

AND PLEASE, YOU DON'T HAVE TO BE SO POLITE TO ME.

HEY YŪSUKE!!

BUT I'M NOT. I'M--

GOTTA GO, SHŌ.

QUIT GOOFING OFF. GET TO WORK.

BYE

AH...

OH...

BUT THE ONES WHO DIDN'T MAKE THE SECOND TEAM WEREN'T EVEN ALLOWED TO PRACTICE.

BECAUSE OF MY HEIGHT, I WAS AUTOMATICALLY PUT WITH THE THIRD TEAM.

ONLY TIME I WAS ALLOWED TO TOUCH THE BALL WAS PRACTICE LIFTING.

ALL I EVER DID WAS RUN ERRANDS, MY DAILY 10 KM JOG.

INCREDIBLE!

HE DID IT OVER 1,000 TIMES!!

HUH?

OOPS!

THAT'S WHY, DAY AFTER DAY...

OVER AND OVER...

IF I GET GOOD AT LIFTING...

IF I GET GOOD AT LIFTING...

...I MIGHT HAVE A CHANCE TO BE MOVED UP.

ER
...

INCREDIBLE.
JUST AS
EXPECTED
FROM
MUSASHI-
NOMORI!

PONG
PONG

PONG

OKAY,
FIVE-ON-
FIVE, A
MINI-GAME
WITH
SHŌ.

I
DIDN'T
MEAN
TO ...

WILL YOU
SHOW US
MUSASHI-
NOMORI'S
TECHNIQUE
DURING A
GAME?

WHAT
?

LET'S PRACTICE
TOGETHER.

HEY,
THAT'S
NO GOOD
...
DON'T
PRACTICE
ALONE
LIKE
THAT
...

BAM

WHISSSTLE

BUT I'LL GIVE
IT A SHOT.

UH-OH,

I HAVEN'T EVEN
PRACTICED YET.

NOD

YOU SHOULDN'T KEEP YOUR CLIENT WAITING, KŌ.

WELL, YEAH.

WHAT DO YOU MEAN, NOTHING?

UMM, YES...

HE'S CUTE. MUST BE A GOOD KID.

DON'T BE A BABY!

WHY DID I TRANSFER SCHOOLS?

TAP

TAP

TAP

IT'S BECAUSE I DIDN'T WANT TO GIVE UP WHO I AM...

...AND BECAUSE I LOVE PLAYING SOCCER.

PAD

PAD

I DIDN'T WANT THEM TO LOSE FAITH IN ME SO FAST.

...THEY'LL ACCEPT ME!

BUT NOW I'VE GOT TO CATCH UP TO THEIR LEVEL BEFORE...

SH-SHŌ...?

WHAMP

...SO WHERE IS--

HE'S NOT AT MY PLACE, AND HE HASN'T GONE BACK TO OUR PARENTS'...

125

NO!! YOU'RE NOT RESPONSIBLE. IT'S ALL MY FAULT...

AND IF THERE'S ANYTHING I CAN DO TO HELP...

ANY-THING?

NO. IT'S MINE. I'M HIS GUARDIAN. I RUN, UMM, A HOST CLUB... AND NOW MY BROTHER IS SUFFERING BECAUSE OF IT...

CITTER CITTER

Wow! Super cool!

Whose brother is he?

SO THAT'S WHAT HAPPENED?

MY THOUGHTLESS CONDUCT HURT YOUR BROTHER'S FEELINGS. IT'S BECAUSE OF ME THAT HE'S NOT IN SCHOOL.

WHAT?

grinnn

... YOU'LL OVERLOOK HIM, WILL YOU?

THEN...

HE GOT ME!

H-HE... MS. KATORI, I KNEW YOU WERE A WONDERFUL WOMAN.

GRINN

Y... YES.

EVEN IF MY BROTHER DOESN'T SHOW UP FOR A LONG TIME, YOU'LL DO EVERYTHING YOU CAN TO KEEP THIS UNDER CONTROL... WON'T YOU?

SO YOU WILL PLEASE REFRAIN FROM SEDUCING MY STUDENTS.

SLEAZE BALL!

JUNIOR HIGH GIRLS ARE QUITE DEVELOPED THESE DAYS, AREN'T THEY?

THEY'RE LIKE ALREADY MATURE WOMEN.

WH-WHAT IS IT?

TEACHER..?

SKREEEKKK

OOOOHHH!

AND WHEN HE DOES, PLEASE LOOK AFTER HIM.

WHATEVER YOU MIGHT HAVE THOUGHT, DESPITE HIS LOOKS, MY BROTHER IS STRONG AT HEART. HE WILL DEFINITELY RETURN TO PLAY SOCCER.

WH-WH-WHA...?

NEXT TIME, LET ME BRING IT AS A GIFT.

YOU'D LOOK BETTER WITH ORANGE COLORED LIPSTICK THAN PINK.

THERE'S SOMETHING ELSE?

OH, AND OF COURSE...

NO! WRONG... THAT'S WRONG! THAT THING ABOUT YESTERDAY...

I MEAN, HE'S SO STUPID FOR LYING ABOUT SOMETHING SO EASY TO DISCOVER. SERVES HIM RIGHT.

TATSUYA!

OH...

TEACHER, IS SHŌ SKIPPING SCHOOL?

WHAT THE HECK? A REAL LOVER BOY, HUH? I DON'T NEED YOUR HELP.

WHIISSHHH

!

WHOOF

WHIISSSHHHH

WHANK

!!

OH! YOU GUYS WANNA PLAY?

IT'S A LOT OF FUN.

OOOHHHHH...

HUHHHH

GGRRRRRR

THIS PARK IS *NOT* YOUR PRIVATE PROPERTY, YOU KNOW...

BLAH BLAH BLAH

AND WHAT'LL YOU DO IF *MY* KIDS GET INJURED BY THE BALL? HUH?

...SO EVEN IF I HAVE TO SKIP SCHOOL, I'VE GOT TO PRACTICE.

THERE WAS NO POINT IN TRANSFERRING SCHOOLS IF I CAN'T PLAY SOCCER....

SPARK EEKKK

KŌ? HE'S NOT HERE.

BUT I HAVE TO TALK TO HIM...

KŌ, I'M HOME--

130

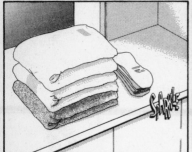

WHAT HAPPENED? ALL OF A SUDDEN...

IT MIGHT SNOW TOMORROW.

EVERY-THING'S NEAT AND CLEAN!

HUH?

Do your best, Shō!!
From your big bro.

IT'S A... SOCCER RICE BALL? IT'S HUGE!

WHAT'S THIS?

WHAT'S INSIDE IT?

KŌ...

131

IT WAS DELICIOUS THANKS-- SHŌ.

SLAM

IT'S BEEN A WEEK...

WHOA!

I ASSUMED HE WAS A REGULAR AND GOT ALL EXCITED WITHOUT CHECKING.

...HE NEVER LIED TO US.

THINKING OF IT...

AWWW, IT WAS A DISGRACE. NO WONDER HE REFUSES TO COME TO SCHOOL.

Y'KNOW, I THOUGHT IT WAS JUST SOCCER, BUT I HEAR HE'S NOT GOING TO CLASSES EITHER.

I HEARD HE WAS SICK AT HOME.

SORRY!

WE'VE ONLY GOT A MONTH BEFORE THE CHAMPIONSHIP BEGINS.

JUST WORRY ABOUT YOUR- SELVES, OKAY?

CHILL OUT.

HUH?

132

...MAYBE EVEN BEYOND THE BRIDGE.

TODAY, I'M GOING TO RUN FURTHER...

!

SHŌ?!

TATSUYA!

THOUGH STILL FAR FROM THE LEVEL EXPECTED FROM MUSASHIN-OMORI.

LOOKS LIKE YOU'VE GOTTEN A BIT BETTER...

TATSUYA...

...

YOU'VE BEEN HAVING A PRETTY HARD TIME, HAVEN'T YOU? I ACTUALLY THOUGHT YOU RAN AWAY.

NO REASON... JUST HAPPENED BY.

WHY ARE YOU HERE?

...

DRIBBLE AND TRY TO GO PAST THE OPPONENT...

ONE-ON-ONE.

WILL YOU PLAY A GAME WITH ME?

SURE.

I'M HOME.

SKKREEKK

I'LL PLAY WITH YOU.

134

DRRILLIPP DRRILLIPP

MY FEINT DIDN'T WORK AGAINST HIM...

BUT I CAN WORK A LOT HARDER...

I MAY BE A LOUSY PLAYER...

AND I'M GONNA STAND ON THE SAME GROUND WITH TATSUYA AND THE OTHERS...

GRRIP

DDRRILLIPP

I COULDN'T GET PAST HIM. NOT EVEN ONCE. I MEAN, I WAS PATHETIC--

YOU...

136

REALLY?

YOU DO?

YOU'RE LYING.

I... GAVE UP FIGHTING.

KŌ, YOU'RE SO COOL. YOU CAN DO ANY- THING...

THERE. IT'S DONE.

SLICK

AND JUST BECAUSE YOU'RE SHORT, WHICH IS AN AWFUL EXCUSE, THEY WOULDN'T LET YOU PLAY...

BUT YOU STILL DIDN'T GIVE UP. YOU TRANSFERRED TO ANOTHER SCHOOL...YOU RISKED BEING DISOWNED BY OUR PARENTS...

MUSASHINOMORI'S KNOWN FOR ACADEMIC AND ATHLETIC EXCELLENCE. YOU WENT TO IT AND YOU MET OUR PARENTS' WISHES TO DO WELL IN YOUR STUDIES. BUT, SHŌ, YOU DIDN'T LET GO OF SOCCER.

LIKE YOU, I HAD A DREAM, BUT IT WAS TOO HARD... I GAVE IT UP.

EVEN THOUGH NOW I SORT OF ENJOY THE JOB....

BUT I STILL REFUSED TO GIVE INTO OUR PARENTS. THAT'S WHY I HAVE THE HOST CLUB.

BUT, YOU'RE DIFFERENT.

I... COULD NEVER FIND THE STRENGTH TO DO THAT.

138

I BELIEVE IN YOU 100 PERCENT!

AND THAT'S WHY I WANT YOU TO TRUST YOUR OWN POWER!

YOU DON'T WANT TO GIVE UP ON YOURSELF, DO YOU?

YOU LOVE PLAYING SOCCER, DON'T YOU?

UH-HUH

SHŌ...

TRUST YOURSELF!

EVEN THOUGH EVERYONE SAID IT WASN'T POSSIBLE, YOU'RE THE MAN WHO WAS ACCEPTED TO MUSASHINOMORI!

WWWIPPPE

I *WON'T* GIVE UP!

GRIIZNNN

FSSH

ESCAPE TOWARD VICTOR

THIS IS IT!

HEH HEH HEH

A SECRET WEAPON?

BRO, YOU'RE ACTING REALLY WEIRD...

WHAT?

GOOD! NOW I'LL GIVE YOU A SECRET WEAPON.

YOU'RE GOOD AT LIFTING, RIGHT?

A FOREIGN MOVIE?

THERE'S SOME SUPER-TECH MOVES HERE YOU SHOULD BE ABLE TO USE.

OF COURSE!

...YEAH, SOMEWHAT.

"LIFTING!" YOU STUDIED SOCCER?

WHOA!

BLAM!

IF YOUR OPPONENT IS A SUPERIOR PLAYER...

... YOU NEED TO POLISH WHAT YOU'RE BEST AT THEN USE IT IN THE FIGHT!

KŌ...

IT'S NOT EASY TO KICK IT UP LIKE THE VIDEO.

AM I HITTING TOO HARD, OR WHAT?

SHARP-LY...

A LOT...

FAST-ER.

...FAST-ER.

USE THE HEEL, SORT OF, AND...

OKAY... JUST RELAX...

TAT-SUYA...

IT'S NO WONDER SINCE I SO COMPLETELY BEAT HIM YESTERDAY...

NOT HERE... HUH.

TAP TAP TAP TAP

142

TO BE CONTINUED IN WHISTLE, VOL.1

Q: Why do YOU want to check out the following titles?
A: Only because they include some of the best manga from Japan, of course!

 page 6

Beet hastily and fearlessly becomes a Level 1 Vandel Buster, attacking monsters and demons who've ushered in the Century of Darkness. His weakness: staying awake for three days then falling into a deep sleep for a full day. This humorous tale is full of action!

 page 94

Too short for the elite soccer team at his previous school, Shô Kazamatsuri thinks he can easily start over and play soccer like he's always wanted to, at his new school. Will changing schools be the answer to his problems? Find out in this lively, goal-tending sports manga!

BLEACH page 51

The story packs a punk rock edge and speaks to fans who love contemporary ghost stories. With so much action, drama and otherworldliness involved, it's hard for anyone to pass up the fast-moving plots and **BLEACH**'s brooding, dark hero Ichigo Kurosaki, who goes after evil spirits to save his own family.

 page 150

This series became the No. 1 sports manga in Japan as soon as it was released. Why? It has a really good-looking young tennis player named Ryoma Echizen at its center. Plus, he must deal with family honor, sports politics and, of course, dynamic moves on the tennis court! With plenty of competition on and off the court, readers are in for some volley action that will whet their appetites for more. Find out why Ryoma must keep defending himself as the Prince of Tennis.

 page 146

Before this manga hit in Japan, people thought of Go as simply a game for senior citizens. Like chess, Go is played in parks on lazy Sunday afternoons over tea or... in tournament settings, with a stop clock and cutthroat rankings. **HIKARU NO GO** starts with Hikaru's chance meeting with Fujiwara-no-Sai, an ancient Go master spirit. Put them together in modern Tokyo and things instantly get strategic — literally!

 page 156

 page 152

SHAMAN KING reflects the world as it truly is: full of different people, races, cultures, religions and spirits! Leading the rainbow coalition of adventures and characters is Yoh Asakura who fights evil with his spirit ally, Amidamaru. It's urban, the story is high-caliber creative and the action-packed flights of fancy are fantastic! It'll be hard not to let head-phones-wearing Yoh, meddling Manta and even unsympathetic Anna influence your life!

RUROUNI KENSHIN's mix of historical samurai action and romantic comedy has made it a well-loved manga series and equally popular anime on Cartoon Network. Himura Kenshin reluc-tantly joins with Kamiya Kaoru's dojo at a critical time in Japan's history and tries to keep the sword arts alive. Will Himura Kenshin end up as a dying breed of assassin or bring back the once respected role of the samurai?

 pages 162-163

 page 158

One of the world's favorite and most read series of all time, **DRAGON BALL** and **DRAGON BALL Z** have influenced artists galore who've tried and failed to capture creator Akira Toriyama's simple but distinctive style. Based on the Chinese "Monkey King" legend, the series quickly took off on its own to span several universes and became a super martial arts sci-fi fantasy. Goku, Vegeta, Trunks and Cell make for an unforgettable stable of chi-powered villains and heroes!.

Wannabe pirate Luffy, through sheer willpower and want, gathers a ragtag crew of odd characters to join him in the search for great treasure along the Grand Line, the most dangerous route on the high seas! Maybe the idea of being the King of the Pirates wouldn't be so far-fetched if Luffy hadn't eaten the Gum-Gum Fruit, which allows him to stretch like rubber, at the cost of never being able to swim again!

 page 168

 page 164

The young orphaned hero of **NARUTO** deals with his coming-of-age period like any other pimple-faced, attention-hungry, happy-go-lucky teen. The only thing is, he's got to deal with learning how to be a ninja too. Talk about tough! He's also in love with Sakura, a fellow ninja cadet who has a crush on their other classmate, Sasuke. All talented in their own right, the three are challenged in the extreme arts of ninjutsu!

Princess Sienna, the Knights of Athena and the order that keeps them bound to each other offers up a romantic, chivalrous setting that is hard to resist. Bloody battles ensue in tournaments to determine the greatest Knight. The setting and the battles make this series equally popular with both male and female readers.

 page 174

 page 170

Shy 10th-grader Yugi spent most of his time alone playing games… until he solved the Millennium Puzzle, a mysterious Egyptian artifact passed down from his grandfather. Possessed by the puzzle, Yugi became Yu-Gi-Oh!, the King of Games, and challenged bullies and criminals to the "Shadow Games"… magical games of life and death! Playing the collectible card game "Duel Monsters," Yugi encounters deadly enemies and worthy rivals!

Even bad boys can have big hearts. Meet Yusuke Urameshi, a kid from the wrong side of the tracks who is quickly headed for juvie until one selfless act changes his life, and he becomes a spirit detective assigned to fight crime! Watch as this rock'n'roll story rumbles along from one adventure to another, with amusing side stories to boot.

One day, Hikaru Shindo finds an old Go board. The instant he sees old bloodstains on it, his life changes forever. Watch as Hikaru and Sai take Japan's Go community by storm!

After Fujiwara-no-Sai, the spirit of a genius Go player, becomes a part of Hikaru's consciousness, the sixth grader finds himself seeking out places to play Go. Not because he really wants to at first, Hikaru only tries to appease Sai to prevent his head from exploding from Sai's whining.

However, as Hikaru begins to play Go, he realizes why Sai loves the game so much. It is on one of these early Go excursions that Hikaru meets Akira Toya, a Go prodigy and son of the Toya Meijin, the best Go player in Japan! With Sai's help, Hikaru easily beats Akira, not once but twice! Needless to say, Akira takes the losses hard and is out for a rematch.

After a couple of tournaments, a school festival and a summer pass, Akira and Hikaru find themselves in middle school. Journey along with them and their competitive classmates, as Sai and the Toya Meijin serve as commanding forces propelling the two youths to face each other yet again... playing the ancient game of Go!

Hikaru Shindo

A normal sixth grader who finds himself dealing with a centuries-old ghost and a board game that's even older.

Fujiwara-no-Sai

The ghost who enters into Hikaru's consciousness. His maudlin personality and his love for Go haven't changed since he died. Sai is always pestering Hikaru to play Go.

Akira Toya

Akira is a Go prodigy and the same age as Hikaru. With Sai's help, Hikaru has beaten Akira twice, causing the budding pro to question his own Go skills.

Kimihiro Tsutsui

More a Go strategist than a passionate player, this middle school student relies on how-to Go books instead of his brains during matches.

Yuki Mitani

A Haze Middle School student who knows how to play Go well. But how well may depend on something other than skill...

Akari Fujisaki

Hikaru's classmate and friend. Akari takes the brunt of Hikaru's bad temper when he doesn't want to explain Go to her.

Topspin excitement in every volume!

THE SERIES THAT BECAME THE NO. 1 SPORTS MANGA IN JAPAN OVERNIGHT!

ALSO A POPULAR ANIME IN JAPAN

- Vol. 3 now available!
- $7.95
- Bimonthly

There's a rumor going around that a 12-year-old boy is entering the 16-and-under age group tennis competition. How can someone so young compete with the big boys? Well, he's no ordinary kid — he's none other than Ryoma Echizen, the Prince of Tennis! Fresh from winning tournaments in the United States, he has come home and enrolled at the top-seed tennis school in the district — Seishun Tennis Academy — where he wows everyone with his unbelievable talent, experience and knowledge of the game. Ryoma's father, Nanjiro, was once an up-and-coming tennis star until an injury ended his tennis days forever. And as Nanjiro's talent was passed on to his son, Ryoma must now battle players from other schools, as well as his own, to prove his reign as the Prince of Tennis!

Winner of four consecutive U.S. Junior championships, Ryoma's cool confidence raises the hackles of a few older students on the tennis team, and they challenge him to a game — but none of them even comes close to the mastery he has over tennis...

Even though rules don't allow seventh graders to participate in the tournaments, the captain has arranged for Ryoma to enter the ranking matches in the city tournament. Ryoma beats two popular team starters to earn the right to play in the district preliminaries. As the youngest (and shortest) player on the team, he looks like one of the upperclassmen's little brothers, but that's only because the public at large has no clue about his level of competency. He becomes the team's secret weapon.

Much to Ryoma's chagrin, Coach Ryuzaki decides to use him for doubles. Ryoma gets paired up with Momo to play No. 1 doubles, and their opponents don't take long to discover their most obvious weakness — lack of teamwork! Brilliant Ryoma hatches a plan to work through their disadvantages, and they slowly but surely turn the situation to their favor. But the challenge isn't over. Fudomine's Team, a rough bunch of players who were disqualified from last year's tournament due to a fighting scandal, are their next opponents...

Sadaharu Inui

Mr. Percentages. Gathers information on tennis players and calculates his chances of winning based on his data.

Kaoru Kaido

The absolute sore loser. Hasn't gotten over losing to Ryoma in the ranking matches held at the start of the school year.

Ryoma Echizen

The Prince of Tennis Seishun Academy's secret weapon.

Shusuke Fuji

One of the first players to recognize Ryoma's unmistakable talent.

Kunimitsu Tezuka

Seishun Academy's cold and enigmatic team captain. Feels threatened by Ryoma's talent and popularity.

Takeshi Momoshiro

Ryoma's doubles partner. Best known for his deadly smash.

Kenshin finds himself as a de facto member of the Kamiya dojo, a school for sword arts that is run by the spirited (and skilled) Kamiya Kaoru. Along with Kaoru, young thief-turned-student Myôjin Yahiko, and reformed street fighter Sagara Sanosuke, Kenshin explores the vibrant new Meiji era, but will he ever be able to escape his bloody past?

Isurugi Raijûta, an old-school swordsman, comes to Kenshin for aid in reforming the state of Japan's swordsmanship schools. Kenshin is intrigued by the idea, but not on board with Raijûta's plans. Given the choice of joining Raijûta's movement or dying, Kenshin walks away, choosing neither. But Raijûta will stop at nothing to ensure the supremacy of his own school of sword-fighting!

Reunited with a member of the former Sekihô Army — a doomed civilian unit — Sanosuke runs into trouble of his own. Old alliances are challenged when a plan to topple the current government by any means necessary is shared… and as his friend puts it, Sano's either "in" or he's "in the way."

Himura Kenshin [Hitokiri Battosai]

Once an assassin named *Battosai*, Kenshin vanished during the final days of pre-Meiji Japan, only to recently surface at the Kamiya dojo. A man of principles and discipline, Kenshin's skill with a sword (either a *katana* or his reversed-edge *sakabatô*) is legendary.

Kamiya Kaoru

Daughter to the founder of the *Kamiya Kasshin-ryû* dojo, Kaoru's brand of sword-fighting rejects the ethics of the *Satsujin-ken* (or "swords that give death"), and instead follows a philosophy akin to the ways of *Katsujin-ken* ("swords that give life"). While her ways are indeed peaceful, her (bad) cooking, on the other hand, can be considered an act of violence.

Sagara Sanosuke [Alias: Zanza]

Until his own fateful run-in with Kenshin and company, Sanosuke subsisted on a healthy diet of fisticuffs and street fighting. A self-proclaimed fighter-for-hire, Sanosuke eventually proves to be one of Kenshin's most formidable allies. Always the skeptic, Sanosuke's brusque manner belies his overall sense of duty.

Myôjin Yahiko

Son of an ex-samurai, Yahiko is rescued from the clutches of a yakuza crime-ring by Kenshin, and thus becomes the former *hitokiri*'s first student. Headstrong and cocky, Yahiko anxiously awaits the day when he too will become a swordsman of repute (until then, he is not above using his skills as a former pickpocket to defeat his unsuspecting enemies).

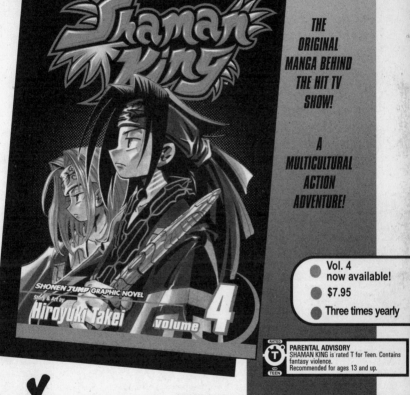

When Manta met his new classmate Yoh, they had one thing in common: they could both see ghosts.

But that was only the beginning, because although Manta had spent most of his life in cram school, Yoh had been trained since birth to contact the dead and use their powers! But with great ghosts comes great responsibility. Using the skills of the samurai Amidamaru, Yoh found himself fighting a power-hungry Chinese shaman, Ren; Lee Bailong, a zombie kung fu master; and Tokagero, the "lizard man," an evil ghost who had fought Amidamaru when he was alive!

But the first chapter of Yoh's life as a shaman has just barely begun. The time has come for the "Shaman Fight in Tokyo," the ultimate tournament battle between every witch, warlock and prophet on Earth. Who are the organizers of the Shaman Fight? What are the rules? Where do you get tickets? Whether he likes it or not, Yoh's questions are about to be answered…

Yoh Asakura

Cheerful and easygoing, Yoh seems to be a slacker, but he is actually the heir to a long line of Japanese shamans. He's engaged to marry Anna, even though they're both in junior high.

Manta Oyamada

A meek student who always carries a huge dictionary. He can see ghosts, but can't use their powers like Yoh and Anna.

Amidamaru

A samurai who died in Japan's Muromachi Era (1334-1467), Amidamaru is Yoh's ghostly companion.

Anna Kyôyama

Yoh's no-nonsense fiancée, she is an *itako* (a traditional Japanese shaman).

Silva

A powerful Native American shaman.

Bokuto No Ryu

Called "Bokuto no Ryu" for the wooden sword he carries, this macho but well-meaning gang boss has the power to see ghosts too.

Adventure on the high seas!

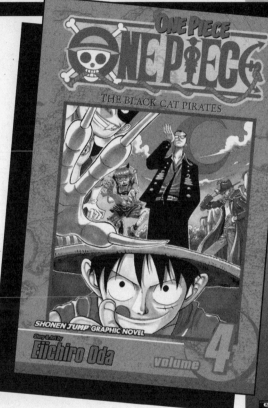

ANIME TO AIR ON FOXBOX IN FALL 2004!

POPULAR, ONGOING SERIES IN JAPAN!

- Vol. 4 now available!
- $7.95
- Three times yearly

When Monkey D. Luffy accidentally ate the cursed Gum-Gum Fruit, he gained the power to stretch like rubber... at the cost of never being able to swim again! Despite this, he's vowed to someday become King of the Pirates and find the legendary treasure known as the "One Piece." Along the way, Luffy picks up several unlikely crewmates and battles a host of exotic and unbelievable sea-going foes.

In the Golden Age of Piracy, countless pirates sail the seas, searching for legendary pirate Gold Roger's mysterious treasure, the "One Piece." Among them is Monkey D. Luffy, who grew up listening to the wild tales of buccaneer "Red-Haired" Shanks and dreaming of becoming a pirate himself. Having accidentally eaten the cursed Devil "Gum-Gum" Fruit as a child, Luffy is able to stretch his body like rubber — at the cost of never being able to swim again.

As Luffy's quest to become King of the Pirates begins, he battles Navy Captain "Axe-Hand" Morgan, helping to free the master swordsman and pirate hunter Roronoa Zolo. In exchange, Zolo joins Luffy's crew.

Next, the two meet up with Nami, an untrustworthy thief and great navigator — together they must outwit and outfight the ruthless pirate clown Captain Buggy, who also possesses mysterious powers connected wth the Devil Fruit.

When Luffy and his unlikely crewmates meet up with Usopp, a small-town liar with big dreams of piracy, they face one of their most devious enemies yet — the clever and completely evil Cap'n Kuro, who is trying to pull a heist that Usopp just can't stand. Luffy's gang has no choice but to step in and help.

"Red-Haired" Shanks

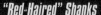

A pirate captain who saved young Luffy's life and inspired him with a love for the sea.

Monkey D. Luffy

Gifted with rubber powers and bottomless optimism, he's determined to become King of the Pirates.

Roronoa Zolo

A former bounty hunter and master of the "three-sword" fighting style — one in each hand and one in his mouth!

Nami

A thief who specializes in robbing pirates. Luffy has convinced her to join his crew as navigator.

Usopp

A village boy with a talent for telling tall tales. He loved claiming to be a pirate captain and annoying the villagers with false pirate warnings... until real pirates landed.

LUFFY AND HIS CREW DEFEND A VILLAGE FROM CAPTAIN KURO AND HIS BLACK CAT PIRATES!
VIZ
ONE PIECE
VOLUME 4!
Only $7.95 Each!
Volumes 1-4 on Sale Now!
Vol. 5 available Nov. 9th!
On Sale At:
www.shonenjump.com
Also available at your local bookstore, comic store and Suncoast Motion Picture Company.
COMIC SHOP LOCATOR SERVICE
888-COMIC-BOOK
888-266-4226
SHONEN JUMP GRAPHIC NOVELS
ONE PIECE © 1997 by EIICHIRO ODA / SHUEISHA Inc. Covers subject to change.

THE INCREDIBLE PREQUEL TO DRAGON BALL Z!

The greatest martial arts manga ever made! From 1984 to 1995, Akira Toriyama's epic *Dragon Ball* thrilled Japanese audiences and set the standard for all manga to come. Now, the entire story of Son Goku is available in English in two parts: *Dragon Ball* (the humorous early years) and *Dragon Ball Z* (the gritty, action-packed later years).

Legend tells that whoever gathers the seven magical "Dragon Balls" will have their wish come true. Son Goku, a young boy from the mountains, first heard the story from a city girl named Bulma, who took him with her on her quest to find the Dragon Balls. Soon, Goku decided that what he really wanted was to be stronger, and so he sought out the world's greatest martial arts masters to show him the ropes. Traveling around the world on his flying cloud, Goku makes friends and fights bad guys on a fantasy adventure.

THE ULTIMATE BATTLE OF KNIGHT AGAINST KNIGHT!

ONE OF JAPAN'S MOST BELOVED ACTION-ADVENTURE FANTASIES!

THE ORIGINAL MANGA BEHIND THE CARTOON NETWORK ANIME!

Ancient myths speak of Athena's Knights, young men of great strength dedicated to defending the goddess Athena. Following their tradition, the mysterious billionaire Lord Nobu sent 100 orphans out into the world to endure brutal combat training. Now the young warriors who survived this ordeal have returned to Japan, carrying the mystical Cloths that are proof of their knighthood. Princess Sienna, the granddaughter of Lord Nobu, announces a grand tournament of the young Knights.

But four Bronze Knights — Pegasus Knight Seiya, Swan Knight Hyôga, Dragon Knight Shiryû and Andromeda Knight Shun — refuse to be used for the entertainment of the rich and powerful. Rebelling against the tournament, they become outlaws, pursued by Knights of incredible power — and find themselves caught in a war between Princess Sienna and Sanctuary, the headquarters of all the Knights of the Zodiac!

Princess Sienna, granddaughter of Lord Nobu, organizes a massive tournament of all the Knights to prove their worth. Among the Knights who join the tournament is Seiya, the Pegasus Knight. Seiya considers the tournament silly and frivolous, but agrees to participate in return for information on the whereabouts of his long-lost sister, Seika.

During the tournament, Phoenix Knight Ikki and his four Black Knights attack and steal the Gold Cloth. Four Bronze Knights — Pegasus Knight Seiya, Swan Knight Hyôga, Dragon Knight Shiryû and Andromeda Knight Shun — set out after them to retrieve the Cloth. At the base of Mount Fuji, they find a labyrinth of caves. There, they face the Black Knights, who are their own dark mirrors.

After battling the Black Knights, the Bronze Knights confront Ikki, a once-kind boy who has been twisted toward hate by his horrific training experiences on Death Queen Island. Horrified by what Ikki has endured, Seiya and his fellow Knights decide that they can no longer tolerate Lord Nobu's cruelty and greed. Instead of killing Ikki, they vow to end the tournament and save their fellow Knights from needless suffering and violence. But Sanctuary, headquarters of all Knighthood, is already planning to put a stop to their rebellion…

Dragon Knight Shiryû

Cool and reserved, Shiryû trained in China and has a tattoo of a Chinese dragon that contains his strength. He is intensely loyal to his friends and will make immense sacrifices for the other Bronze Knights.

Swan Knight Hyôga

Hyôga trained in Siberia, where his mother died in a shipwreck. He wishes to spend his life there, swimming to the bottom of the ocean each morning to lay a flower on his mother's resting place. His reasons for returning to Japan are still veiled in secrecy.

Pegasus Knight Seiya

Trained in Greece, Seiya won the Pegasus Cloth after mastering his signature move, the Meteor Punch. He is brave, energetic and often hot-headed. He returns to Japan in search of his missing sister.

Andromeda Knight Shun

Young, delicate and sensitive, Shun is nonetheless a skilled fighter, using the Andromeda Chains on his armor as formidable weapons. Before being sent to train on Andromeda Island, he was very close to his older brother Ikki, who protected him from harm.

Phoenix Knight Ikki

Ikki was a kind boy, devoted to his brother Shun, before he was sent to train on the terrible Death Queen Island. His experiences there turned him into a bitter killer. Now he dreams of destroying everything associated with Lord Nobu and Knighthood — even his brother!

Naruto is assigned to a three-student cell, along with feisty Sakura and brooding Sasuke, and taught by advanced ninja Kakashi, a mentor as well as instructor. Tired of easy exercises, Naruto and his classmates make the mistake of asking Kakashi for a really hard assignment... and find themselves in the Land of Waves, protecting a bridge-builder named Tazuna. But the job turns truly dangerous when the notorious assassin Zabuza shows up. While Kakashi holds off Zabuza and Sakura protects Tazuna, Naruto and Sasuke face Zabuza's assistant Haku.

In the battle, Sasuke makes a big sacrifice to save Naruto from Haku's deadly throwing needles. For Naruto, watching Sasuke fall causes something terrible to stir within him as rage awakens the nine-tailed fox spirit. He now has the strength to overcome the assassin Haku — but can he bring himself to finish the job?

As the battle for the Land of the Waves comes to a tragic ending, our heroes return to the village of Konohagakure in time for the chûnin (journeyman ninja) exams. Junior ninja from around the world have gathered to take the exam, bringing their own strange forms of ninjutsu and the will to advance to the next level... at any cost!

Naruto

When Naruto was an infant, a destructive fox spirit was imprisoned inside his body. Spurned by the elders of his village, this impish orphan has grown into an attention-seeking troublemaker. His goal: to become the village's next Hokage.

Sasuke

The top student in Naruto's class, Sasuke comes from the prestigious Uchiha clan. His goal: to get revenge on a mysterious person who wronged him in the past.

Sakura

Smart and studious, Sakura is the brightest of Naruto's classmates, but she's constantly distracted by her crush on Sasuke. Her goal: to win Sasuke's heart!

Kakashi

The elite ninja assigned to train Naruto, Sasuke and Sakura. His Sharingan ("Mirror-Wheel Eye") allows him to reflect and mimic enemy ninjutsu.

Haku

A mysterious orphan who befriends Naruto. Naruto doesn't realize that his new friend is Zabuza's loyal masked assistant, who fights with acupuncture needles.

Zabuza

A ruthless ninja assassin and mass-murderer known as "The Demon." He specializes in techniques involving water and mist.

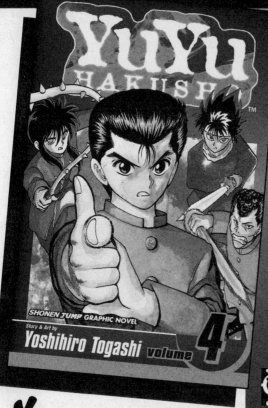

At the brink of defeat against wicked Suzaku, Yusuke suddenly felt a surge of renewed power that allowed him to destroy the enchanted whistle, but left him completely drained afterwards. Yusuke and Kurama managed to revive their comrades, but later Keiko pressured Yusuke into promising to make her the first to know whenever he gets sent on another dangerous mission. Back in the Underworld, Urameshi and Kuwabara's half-human and half-demon impostors prepared for a showdown at an abandoned hell housing development site, but Hiei quickly squashed them and their team of diabolical half-breeds.

As Kuwabara falls in love with the Ice Maiden, a non-human girl in distress at the hands of pug-ugly gem dealer Gonzo Tarukane, an adventure in the Underworld becomes inevitable. After being captured and held hostage for her unique ability to produce exquisite jewelry from her own tears, the Ice Maiden lived as a prisoner at Tarukane's summer mansion. Enter Urameshi and Kuwabara, who tackle Tarukane's security men — the Toguro Brothers, otherwise known as the Brokers of Darkness. Kuwabara makes it his personal mission to slay demon after demon to restore her freedom.

Yusuke Urameshi

The toughest student at Sarayashiki Junior High — until his untimely death. Now he's finally rejoined the world of the living.

Botan

The ferrywoman of the Sanzu River (the River Styx in Western mythology). Guided Yusuke through his trials in the afterlife.

Keiko Yukimura

Yusuke's childhood friend. She cared for his comatose body while he was dead and delivered the kiss that returned him to life.

Koenma

The son of King Enma, Lord of the Underworld. He runs the spirit world while his father is away.

Kuwabara

Another Sarayashiki delinquent, and Yusuke's chief rival. An encounter with the ghostly Yusuke awakened untapped psychic powers within him.

Atsuko Urameshi

Yusuke's loving but flaky mom, who's better at partying than looking after her delinquent son.

LET THE SHADOW GAMES BEGIN!

THE ORIGINAL MANGA BEHIND THE POPULAR TV SHOW!

A HIT CARD GAME AND VIDEO GAME SERIES!

SHONEN JUMP GRAPHIC NOVEL

Story & Art by
Kazuki Takahashi

volume **6**

Shy and easily picked on, 10th grader Yugi spent his time alone playing games... until he solved the Millennium Puzzle, a mysterious Egyptian artifact passed down from his grandfather. Possessed by the power of the puzzle, Yugi became Yu-Gi-Oh!, the King of Games, a dark avenger of justice who challenges evildoers to weird games where the losers lose their minds!

When Yugi solved the Millennium Puzzle, his life changed forever. While Yugi's original personality slept, "Dark Yugi" took over his body and dealt gamer justice to bullies, criminals and frauds.

But the mystery of the Millennium Puzzle brought Yugi enemies as well as friends. Shadi, an Egyptian sorcerer, put Yugi through a series of tests to see if he was worthy of wielding the ancient power of his homeland. Then Seto Kaiba, megalomaniacal card game champion, forced Yugi into a collectible card game match with the life of Yugi's grandfather at stake. Each time, Yugi has come out triumphant, but can his winning streak go on forever? Against tough new opponents and strange new games, can Yugi protect his friends… or even himself?

YUGI MUTOU
DARK YUGI (YAMI YUGI)

The main character. When he solved the ancient Egyptian Millennium Puzzle, he developed an alter ego, Yami Yugi (Dark Yugi), which emerges in times of stress.

KATSUYA JONOUCHI

Yugi's classmate, a tough guy who gets in a lot of fights. He used to think Yugi was a wimp, but now they are good friends. In the English anime he's known as "Joey Wheeler."

ANZU MAZAKI

Yugi's classmate and childhood friend. Her first name means "Peach." In the English anime she's known as "Téa Gardner."

HIROTO HONDA

Yugi's classmate, a friend of Jonouchi. In the English anime he's known as "Tristan Taylor."

SETO KAIBA

The revenge-obsessed heir to a multimillion-dollar gaming empire. He spent $80 million to build the "Theme Park of Death" to kill Yugi and his friends.

RYO BAKURA

A transfer student at Yugi's school, he possesses the mysterious Millennium Ring.

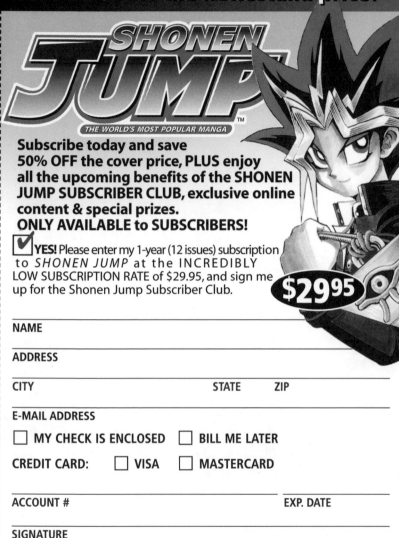

COMPLETE OUR SURVEY AND LET US KNOW WHAT YOU THINK!

☐ Please do NOT send me information about VIZ and SHONEN JUMP products, news and events, special offers, or other information.

☐ Please do NOT send me information from VIZ's trusted business partners.

Name: _____

Address: _____

City: _____ State: _____ Zip: _____

E-mail: _____

☐ Male ☐ Female   Date of Birth (mm/dd/yyyy): ___ / ___ / ___   (Under 13? Parental consent required)

What race/ethnicity do you consider yourself? (please check one)

☐ Asian/Pacific Islander ☐ Black/African American ☐ Hispanic/Latino

☐ Native American/Alaskan Native ☐ White/Caucasian ☐ Other: _____

What SHONEN JUMP Graphic Novel did you purchase? (indicate title purchased)

_____

What other SHONEN JUMP Graphic Novels, if any, do you own? (indicate title(s) owned)

_____

_____

Reason for purchase: (check all that apply)

☐ Special offer ☐ Favorite title ☐ Gift

☐ Recommendation ☐ Read in SHONEN JUMP Magazine

☐ Read excerpt in the SHONEN JUMP Compilation Edition

☐ Other _____

Where did you make your purchase? (please check one)

☐ Comic store ☐ Bookstore ☐ Mass/Grocery Store

☐ Newsstand ☐ Video/Video Game Store ☐ Other: _____

☐ Online (site: _____)

Do you read SHONEN JUMP Magazine?

☐ Yes ☐ No **(if no, skip the next two questions)**

Do you subscribe?

☐ Yes ☐ No

If you do not subscribe, how often do you purchase SHONEN JUMP Magazine?

☐ 1-3 issues a year

☐ 4-6 issues a year

☐ more than 7 issues a year

What genre of manga would you like to read as a SHONEN JUMP Graphic Novel?
(please check two)

☐ Adventure ☐ Comic Strip ☐ Science Fiction ☐ Fighting

☐ Horror ☐ Romance ☐ Fantasy ☐ Sports

Which do you prefer? (please check one)

☐ Reading right-to-left

☐ Reading left-to-right

Which do you prefer? (please check one)

☐ Sound effects in English

☐ Sound effects in Japanese with English captions

☐ Sound effects in Japanese only with a glossary at the back

THANK YOU! Please send the completed form to:

VIZ Survey
42 Catharine St.
Poughkeepsie, NY 12601

SHONEN JUMP CHECKLIST

SHONEN JUMP GRAPHIC NOVELS

BEET THE VANDEL BUSTER
- [ ] Vol. 1

W9-CXY-569

BLEACH
- [ ] Vol. 1
- [ ] Vol. 2
- [ ] Vol. 3

DRAGON BALL
- [ ] Vol. 1
- [ ] Vol. 2
- [ ] Vol. 3
- [ ] Vol. 4
- [ ] Vol. 5
- [ ] Vol. 6
- [ ] Vol. 7
- [ ] Vol. 8
- [ ] Vol. 9
- [ ] Vol. 10
- [ ] Vol. 11
- [ ] Vol. 12
- [ ] Vol. 13
- [ ] Vol. 14
- [ ] Vol. 15
- [ ] Vol. 16

DRAGON BALL Z
- [ ] Vol. 1
- [ ] Vol. 2
- [ ] Vol. 3
- [ ] Vol. 4
- [ ] Vol. 5
- [ ] Vol. 6
- [ ] Vol. 7
- [ ] Vol. 8
- [ ] Vol. 9
- [ ] Vol. 10
- [ ] Vol. 11
- [ ] Vol. 12
- [ ] Vol. 13
- [ ] Vol. 14
- [ ] Vol. 15
- [ ] Vol. 16
- [ ] Vol. 17

HIKARU NO GO
- [ ] Vol. 1
- [ ] Vol. 2

NARUTO
- [ ] Vol. 1
- [ ] Vol. 2
- [ ] Vol. 3
- [ ] Vol. 4

ONE PIECE
- [ ] Vol. 1
- [ ] Vol. 2
- [ ] Vol. 3
- [ ] Vol. 4

THE PRINCE OF TENNIS
- [ ] Vol. 1
- [ ] Vol. 2
- [ ] Vol. 3

RUROUNI KENSHIN
- [ ] Vol. 1
- [ ] Vol. 2
- [ ] Vol. 3
- [ ] Vol. 4
- [ ] Vol. 5
- [ ] Vol. 6
- [ ] Vol. 7

SHAMAN KING
- [ ] Vol. 1
- [ ] Vol. 2
- [ ] Vol. 3
- [ ] Vol. 4

YU-GI-OH!
- [ ] Vol. 1
- [ ] Vol. 2
- [ ] Vol. 3
- [ ] Vol. 4
- [ ] Vol. 5
- [ ] Vol. 6

YUYU HAKUSHO
- [ ] Vol. 1
- [ ] Vol. 2
- [ ] Vol. 3
- [ ] Vol. 4

WHISTLE!
- [ ] Vol. 1

SHONEN JUMP ADVANCED GRAPHIC NOVELS

ULTIMATE MUSCLE
- [ ] Vol. 1
- [ ] Vol. 2

SHONEN JUMP MAGAZINE

- [ ] **12 ACTION-PACKED ISSUES FOR JUST $29.95**

Call 1-800-541-7919
or visit www.shonenjump.com

CLIP AND TAKE WITH YOU

THE WORLD'S MOST POPULAR MANGA

SHONEN JUMP GRAPHIC NOVELS